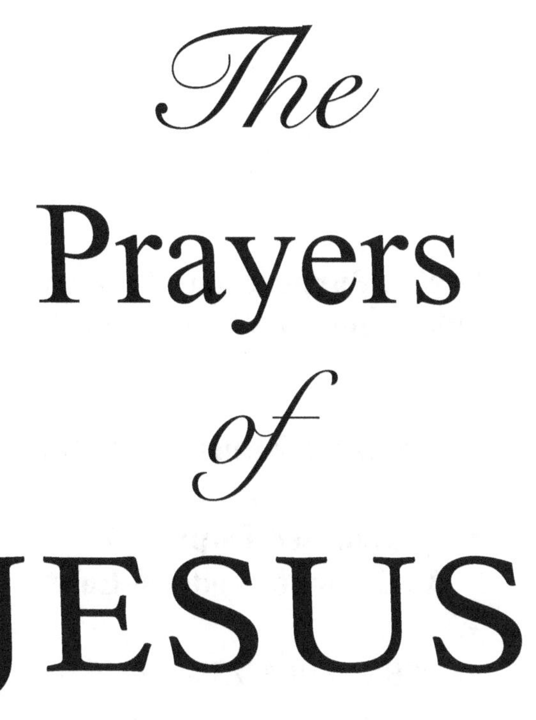

How the Power, Purpose, and Pattern of Christ's Prayer Life Can Transform Yours

by SONJIA B. DICKERSON

How the Power, Purpose, and Pattern of Christ's Prayer Life Can Transform Yours

ISBN: 978-1-7330235-8-0

Printed in the United States

Dedication

To my husband Bishop Kevin K. Dickerson As this books reflects on the prayers of Jesus, I thank God for a man whose own prayers have strengthened, covered, and guided our family. I have so much love and respect for you.

To my Sister Missionary Mary Reaves – My #1 Prayer Warrior and Friend.

To every believer who wants a deeper relation-ship with God through prayer. May your time with Him transform your life, your family, and your calling.

Table of Contents

THE PRAYERS OF JESUS

How the Power, Purpose, and Pattern of Christ's Prayer Life Can Transform Your Prayer Life

FOREWORD

Prayer is not merely a religious exercise—it is the lifeline of the believer. In a generation filled with noise, distraction, and spiritual fatigue, the call to prayer has never been more urgent. Yet many believers struggle not with the desire to pray, but with understanding how to pray effectively.

This book invites you into the sacred prayer life of Jesus Christ. Not as a distant theological concept, but as a living pattern to be followed, embraced, and experienced. The prayers of Jesus are not accidental moments—they are intentional revelations. They show us how heaven responds when earth prays correctly.

What you hold in your hands is more than a study—it is a transformation guide.

Prayer has always been heaven's chosen pathway for earthly transformation. Every major move of God in Scripture was preceded, sustained, or birthed through prayer. From the cries of Abraham to the intercession of Moses... from the tears of Hannah to the petitions of David... from the fire on Elijah's altar to the upper room outpouring in Acts—God has always responded to people who know how to seek Him.

Yet among all the examples of prayer in Scripture, none are more powerful, more revealing, or more transformational than the prayers of Jesus Christ.

Jesus did not merely teach prayer.

He embodied prayer.

Prayer was not simply something He practiced.

Prayer was part of His identity.

When the disciples watched Jesus minister, they saw miracles.

They saw blind eyes opened.

They saw demons cast out.

They saw storms obey.

They saw bread multiplied.

They saw the dead raised.

Yet remarkably, they never said:

“Lord, teach us to work miracles.”

They never said:

“Lord, teach us to lead.”

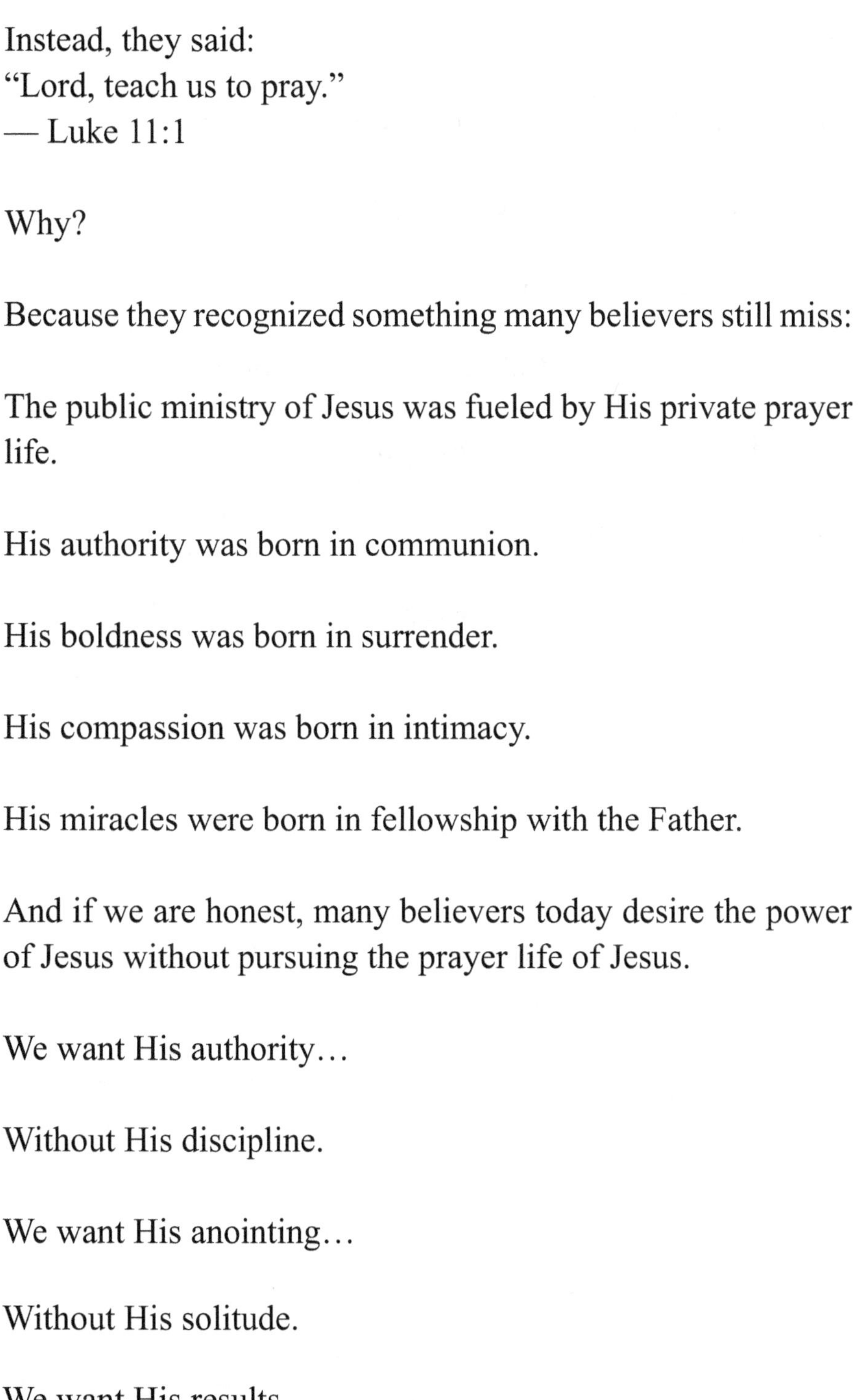

Instead, they said:
"Lord, teach us to pray."
— Luke 11:1

Why?

Because they recognized something many believers still miss:

The public ministry of Jesus was fueled by His private prayer life.

His authority was born in communion.

His boldness was born in surrender.

His compassion was born in intimacy.

His miracles were born in fellowship with the Father.

And if we are honest, many believers today desire the power of Jesus without pursuing the prayer life of Jesus.

We want His authority…

Without His discipline.

We want His anointing…

Without His solitude.

We want His results…

Without His surrender.

But this book is an invitation to something deeper.

This is not simply a book about prayer.

This is a book about transformation.

Because if you truly study the prayer life of Jesus…

You will never pray the same again.

And if you never pray the same again…

You will never live the same again.

INTRODUCTION

Prayer is one of the most precious gifts the Christian receives. The ability to communicate with God is nothing short of amazing. What an honor to share our innermost thoughts, desires, and even insecurities in such an intimate way with the Creator of the universe.

Prayer is not simply thinking about God—it is addressing Him.

It is the engagement of the whole person: mind, body, emotion, and spirit. True prayer is not performance; it is participation in divine fellowship. It is where vulnerability meets sovereignty. It is where humanity encounters divinity.

Prayer is:
- A place of safety
- A place of pain
- A place of joy
- A place of resolution
- A place of challenge

Often, it is all of these at once.

We bring our problems to the One who solves.

We bring our questions to the One who answers.

We bring our lives to the One who gives life.

Prayer is a conversation:

Talk a while.

Listen a while.

Then listen more than you talk.

Because every answer we need is found in what God says back.

As it has been written:

“The child learns to speak because his father speaks to him… So we learn to speak to God because God has spoken to us.”

Even Jesus prayed.

This truth alone reshapes everything. If the Son of God—perfect, sinless, divine—needed prayer, then prayer is not optional for us. It is essential.

This book examines three powerful moments in the life of Christ:

- Jesus Prays at Lazarus’ Grave
- Jesus Prays in Gethsemane
- Jesus Prays on the Cross

Each prayer reveals:

- **The Circumstances** (what surrounded the prayer)
- **The Substance** (what was actually prayed)
- **The Outcome** (what happened because of it)

From these, we will discover **the Power**, **the Purpose**, and **the Pattern** of a transformed prayer life.

WHY STUDY THE PRAYERS OF JESUS?

Many books have been written about prayer.

Many sermons have been preached about prayer.

Many conferences have centered around prayer.

Yet one of the greatest ways to understand prayer is not merely by studying principles…

But by studying a Person.

And that Person is Jesus Christ.

If anyone knew how heaven operates…

It was Jesus.

If anyone understood the heart of the Father…

It was Jesus.

If anyone knew how to pray with authority…

It was Jesus.

And yet, the mystery is this:

Though Jesus was fully God…

He still prayed as fully man.

This is one of the greatest revelations in Scripture.

Jesus did not rely on His divinity to bypass prayer.

He relied on His relationship with the Father through prayer.

That means prayer was not optional for Him.

It was essential.

This should deeply challenge us.

If Jesus prayed before major decisions…

Why do we make decisions without prayer?

If Jesus prayed before ministry…

Why do we serve without prayer?

If Jesus prayed under pressure…

Why do we panic under pressure?

If Jesus prayed through suffering…

Why do we often withdraw from God in suffering?

Prayer was never designed to be a religious duty.

Prayer is relational dependency.

Prayer is the acknowledgment that:

I cannot do this without God.

Prayer says:

My wisdom is not enough.

My strength is not enough.

My resources are not enough.

My gifting is not enough.

I need God.

And the beautiful truth is this:

God delights in being needed.

THE THREE DIMENSIONS OF EVERY PRAYER

As you move through this book, you will discover that every prayer Jesus prayed contained three dimensions:

1. Relationship

Every prayer began with connection.

“Father…”

“Abba…”

“My God…”

Jesus never approached prayer as a stranger.

He approached prayer as a Son.

And because of Christ, we can too.

The Holy Bible Romans 8:15 says:

“Ye have received the Spirit of adoption, whereby we cry, Abba, Father.”

Prayer is not approaching a judge.

Prayer is approaching your Father.

2. Revelation

Jesus prayed according to what He knew about the Father.

He knew:

The Father hears.

The Father sees.

The Father speaks.

The Father sends.

The Father strengthens.

The Father answers.

You cannot pray beyond your revelation of God.

If you see Him as distant…

You will pray timidly.

If you see Him as angry…

If you see Him as faithful…

You will pray boldly.

3. Response

Every prayer Jesus prayed produced movement.

Sometimes immediately.

Sometimes progressively.

Sometimes visibly.

Sometimes invisibly.

But heaven always responded.

And heaven still responds

Prayer is:

- A place of safety
- A place of pain
- A place of joy
- A place of resolution
- A place of challenge

Often, it is all of these at once.

We bring our problems to the One who solves.

We bring our questions to the One who answers.

We bring our lives to the One who gives life.

Prayer is a conversation:

Talk a while.

Listen a while.

Then listen more than you talk.

Because every answer we need is found in what God says back.

As it has been written:

“The child learns to speak because his father speaks to him…

So we learn to speak to God because God has spoken to us.”

Even Jesus prayed.

This truth alone reshapes everything. If the Son of God—perfect, sinless, divine—needed prayer, then prayer is not optional for us. It is essential.

This book examines three powerful moments in the life of Christ:

• Jesus Prays at Lazarus’ Grave

• Jesus Prays in Gethsemane

• Jesus Prays on the Cross

Each prayer reveals:

- The Circumstances (what surrounded the prayer)
- The Substance (what was actually prayed)
- The Outcome (what happened because of it)

From these, we will discover the Power, the Purpose, and the Pattern of a transformed prayer life.

Chapter 1

The Power of Prayer: Jesus at Lazarus' Grave

Scripture Foundation (KJV)

"Then they took away the stone from the place where the dead was laid. And Jesus lifted up his eyes, and said, Father, I thank thee that thou hast heard me.
And I knew that thou hearest me always: but because of the people which stand by I said it, that they may believe that thou hast sent me."
— John 11:41–42

1. The Painful Circumstances Surrounding the Prayer

Jesus stood at a gravesite—but not just any grave.

This was Lazarus.

A friend.

A confidant.

A man Jesus loved deeply.

Scripture confirms this intimacy:

"Lord, behold, he whom thou lovest is sick." (John 11:3)

This was not distant ministry—this was personal loss.

When Jesus arrived, Lazarus had already been dead four days. The atmosphere was thick with grief, disappointment, and even quiet frustration.

Martha said:

"Lord, if thou hadst been here, my brother had not died." (John 11:21)

Mary echoed the same.

The unspoken tension was clear:

"Why didn't You come sooner?"

Jesus was surrounded by:
• Mourning friends
• Confused disciples
• Questioning faith
• And the finality of death

Then comes the shortest verse in the Bible:

"Jesus wept." (John 11:35)

This is critical.

It reveals that prayer is not reserved for composed moments—it is necessary in emotional ones.

Jesus did not avoid the moment.

He entered it fully—and then He prayed.

THE TEARS OF JESUS

"Jesus wept."
— John 11:35

Two words.

Yet they hold oceans of revelation.

These are not the tears of weakness.

These are not the tears of defeat.

These are not the tears of hopelessness.

These are the tears of divine compassion.

The Greek language used here suggests deep emotion—an inward stirring that moved Jesus profoundly.

Jesus was not crying because He lacked power.

He already knew Lazarus would rise.

He had already declared:

"This sickness is not unto death, but for the glory of God."
— John 11:4

So why did He cry?

1. He Wept Because Love Feels Pain

Love does not become emotionless.

Love enters suffering.

Love steps into brokenness.

Love refuses to remain distant.

Jesus did not stand back and say:

"Stop crying—I'm about to fix this."

No.

He entered their pain first.

This is ministry.

Many believers want to fix people before they feel people.

But Jesus teaches us:

Before you speak power…

Feel compassion.

Before you work miracles…

Touch pain.

Before you preach sermons…

Love people.

2. He Wept Because Death Was Never God's Original Design

Every funeral…

Every hospital room…

Every goodbye…

Every cemetery…

Is a reminder that sin changed creation.

Death is an intruder.

Death is an enemy.

The Holy Bible I Corinthians 15:26 says:

"The last enemy that shall be destroyed is death."

Jesus stood before the consequences of sin…

And He wept.

But He did not just weep.

He confronted.

That is the difference between worldly sympathy and kingdom compassion.

Sympathy says:

"I'm sorry."

Compassion says:

"I'm here—and something is about to change."

2. The Power-Filled Substance of the Prayer

What Jesus prayed is astonishing.

He did not begin with:

"Father, raise Lazarus."

Instead, He said:

"Father, I thank thee…"

This is the power principle:

Jesus prayed from assurance, not desperation.

He thanked God before the miracle happened.

This reveals three key truths:

A. Prayer That Believes Before It Sees

Jesus said:

"Thou hast heard me."

Not "hear me now"—but "You already heard me."

Faith speaks in past tense confidence.

B. Prayer That Seeks God's Glory, Not Personal Credit

"That they may believe that thou hast sent me."

Jesus was not performing—He was revealing.

True prayer is not about being seen as powerful.

It is about pointing others to God's power.

C. Prayer That Pauses Before Action

Jesus could have immediately called Lazarus out.

But He stopped… and prayed.

This is a warning:

Never become so busy doing God's work that you stop talking to God.

3. The Powerful Outcome of the Prayer

REMOVE THE STONE

Jesus then gives an unusual command:

"Take ye away the stone."
— John 11:39

Notice:

Jesus had resurrection power.

But He still involved people.

This reveals a profound kingdom principle:

God often does supernaturally what we cannot do…

After we do naturally what we can do.

They could not resurrect Lazarus.

But they could move a stone.

Many believers are praying for God to do what God is waiting for them to do.

Move the stone.

Move:

The stone of bitterness.

The stone of fear.

The stone of procrastination.

The stone of unforgiveness.

The stone of compromise.

The stone of unbelief.

Sometimes the miracle is waiting…

On the other side of your obedience

After praying, Jesus cried:

"Lazarus, come forth." (John 11:43)

And the impossible happened.

A dead man walked out of a grave.

But notice—there were two responses:

A. Some Believed

Faith was ignited.

Lives were changed.

B. Others Plotted to Kill Jesus

"Then from that day forth they took counsel together for to put him to death." (John 11:53)

Here is a mature truth:

Answered prayer does not eliminate opposition—it often intensifies it.

4. The Transformational Pattern for Us

From this moment, we learn:

Pray in Pain

Don't wait until you feel strong—pray when you feel broken.

Pray with Gratitude

Thank God before the answer shows up.

Pray for God's Glory

Make His name the focus, not your outcome.

Pray Before You Act

Even when you "know what to do."

Chapter Reflection Questions

1. What situations in your life feel "dead" right now?

2. Are your prayers driven more by fear or by faith?

3. Do you thank God before or only after He answers?

4. Are you seeking results—or God's glory?

Chapter Prayer

Father,

Teach me to pray like Jesus.

When I face situations that seem beyond repair, help me to trust You before I see results.

Give me the faith to thank You in advance, the humility to seek Your glory, and the discipline to pause and pray.

Revive every dead place in my life according to Your will.

In Jesus' name, Amen.

Chapter 2

The Pupose of Prayer:

Jesus

in

Gethsemane

Scripture Foundation (KJV)

"And he went forward a little, and fell on the ground, and prayed that, if it were possible, the hour might pass from him. And he said, Abba, Father, all things are possible unto thee; take away this cup from me: nevertheless not what I will, but what thou wilt."
— Mark 14:35–36

1. The Pressure-Filled Circumstances Surrounding the Prayer

The Garden of Gethsemane is not a peaceful devotional setting—it is a battlefield.

The name Gethsemane means "oil press," and that is exactly what Jesus experienced. He was being pressed on every side—emotionally, spiritually, and physically.

He had just finished the Last Supper. Betrayal was already in motion. Judas was on his way. The cross was no longer a distant prophecy—it was an imminent reality.

Jesus knew:

- He would be beaten
- He would be mocked
- He would be crucified
- He would carry the sins of the entire world.

But even deeper than physical suffering was the reality of spiritual separation.

For the first time in eternity, the Son would bear sin.

Scripture declares:

"For he hath made him to be sin for us, who knew no sin; that we might be made the righteousness of God in him." (II Corinthians 5:21)

This moment was not just about pain—it was about purpose.

Jesus took Peter, James, and John with Him, but even His closest disciples could not fully carry what He was facing.

"And he saith unto them, My soul is exceeding sorrowful unto death: tarry ye here, and watch." (Mark 14:34)

Then He went further alone.

There are places in prayer where no one can go with you.

THE PRESSURE OF THE PRESS

Gethsemane means "oil press."

In biblical times, olives were crushed under tremendous pressure until oil flowed.

This is not accidental.

This garden was not merely a location.

It was a revelation.

Before Jesus would pour out His life…

He first had to be pressed.

Before oil flows…

Pressure comes.

Before anointing manifests…

Crushing often happens.

Before public ministry reaches its highest expression…

Private surrender must reach its deepest level.

This is where many believers become discouraged.

We often interpret pressure as abandonment.

We assume difficulty means God has left us.

We conclude that opposition means we missed God.

But sometimes pressure is not punishment.

Sometimes pressure is preparation.

Sometimes pressure is proof that something valuable is being produced within you.

Oil only comes from what has been crushed.

Anointing often comes from what has been surrendered.

Character is formed under pressure.

Faith is revealed under pressure.

Prayer deepens under pressure.

Jesus was not in Gethsemane because He was out of God's will.

He was in Gethsemane because He was perfectly in God's will.

That is a word many believers need.

Being in God's will does not exempt you from pressure.

Sometimes it guarantees it.

WHEN YOUR SOUL FEELS OVERWHELMED

Jesus said:

"My soul is exceeding sorrowful unto death…"
— Mark 14:34

Notice this carefully.

Jesus did not deny His emotional pain.

He acknowledged it.

He verbalized it.

He brought it into prayer.

This destroys the myth that spiritual maturity means emotional suppression.

Some believers think faith means pretending.

Pretending you are not hurt.

Pretending you are not tired.

Pretending you are not struggling.

Pretending you are not overwhelmed.

But Jesus shows us another way.

Faith is not denial.

Faith is honesty surrendered to God.

You can be spiritual and still feel pressure.

You can be anointed and still feel sorrow.

You can be called and still feel overwhelmed.

You can be chosen and still cry.

You can be used by God and still need prayer.

Jesus teaches us that vulnerability before God is not weakness.

It is worship.

THE SWEAT LIKE BLOOD

Luke gives us additional insight.

"And being in an agony he prayed more earnestly: and his sweat was as it were great drops of blood falling down to the ground."
— Luke 22:44

This is one of the most intense prayer moments in all Scripture.

The word agony suggests intense struggle.

Deep conflict.

Extreme emotional distress.

Yet notice what Jesus did in agony:

He prayed more earnestly.

Not less.

Pain did not silence prayer.

Pain intensified prayer.

This is a powerful principle.

Pressure should not reduce your prayer.

Pressure should deepen your prayer.

Some people pray until pressure comes.

Jesus prayed because pressure came.

Many people pray until life gets difficult.

Jesus prayed more when life got difficult.

And that is where true spiritual maturity is revealed.

HEAVEN SENT STRENGTH

"And there appeared an angel unto him from heaven, strengthening him."
— Luke 22:43

This is powerful.

The Father did not remove the cup.

But He sent strength.

This is one of the greatest lessons in prayer.

Sometimes God changes circumstances.

Sometimes God changes timelines.

Sometimes God changes people.

But sometimes…

God changes you.

Sometimes the answer is not removal.

Sometimes the answer is reinforcement.

Sometimes the answer is not escape.

Sometimes the answer is empowerment.

Many believers have been praying:

"Lord, get me out."

But heaven may be saying:

"I am making you stronger."

Because sometimes strength is a greater miracle than escape.

THE POWER OF "NEVERTHELESS"

"Nevertheless not what I will, but what thou wilt."
— Mark 14:36
This may be one of the most powerful words in all of Scripture.

Nevertheless.

One word.

One surrender.

One decision.

One alignment.

One death to self.

One yes to God.

Everything changed after "nevertheless."

Destiny moved after "nevertheless."

Redemption moved after "nevertheless."

The cross moved after "nevertheless."

And many lives are waiting on your "nevertheless."

Your ministry.

Your family.

Your healing.

Your obedience.

Your calling.

Your breakthrough.

Your destiny.

Sometimes the greatest spiritual victories are hidden inside one surrendered word:

Nevertheless.

2. The Agonizing Substance of the Prayer

"And he went forward a little, and fell on the ground…"

Jesus didn't kneel politely—He fell.

This was desperation.

This was intensity.

This was total surrender.

A. The Intimacy of Address: "Abba, Father"

"And he said, Abba, Father…"

"Abba" is an intimate term—like "Daddy."

Even in agony, Jesus did not lose intimacy.

This reveals a powerful truth:

Pain should not push you away from God—it should pull you closer.

B. The Acknowledgment of God's Power

"All things are possible unto thee…"

Jesus affirms God's sovereignty.

He recognizes:

There is nothing God cannot do.

Faith does not deny reality—but it declares God's authority over it.

C. The Honest Expression of Desire

"Take away this cup from me…"

Jesus did not hide His feelings.

He was transparent.

The "cup" represents suffering, judgment, and divine wrath.

Jesus, in His humanity, did not desire the suffering—but He did not sin in expressing it.

This gives us permission:
You can be honest in prayer without being rebellious.

D. The Ultimate Surrender

"Nevertheless not what I will, but what thou wilt."

This is the heart of prayer.

Not getting your will done in heaven—

But submitting your will to heaven.

True prayer is not about control—it is about surrender.

3. The Repetition of Prayer and the Weakness of Men

Jesus prayed this prayer multiple times.

"And again he went away, and prayed, and spake the same words." (Mark 14:39)

This was not lack of faith—it was depth of burden.

Meanwhile, the disciples slept.

"And he cometh, and findeth them sleeping, and saith unto

Peter, Simon, sleepest thou? couldest not thou watch one hour?" (Mark 14:37)

Then comes a powerful principle:

"Watch ye and pray, lest ye enter into temptation. The spirit truly is ready, but the flesh is weak." (Mark 14:38)

Prayer is the bridge between a willing spirit and weak flesh.

4. The Outcome: Strength to Fulfill Purpose

After prayer, something shifted.

Jesus did not escape the cross—

But He was strengthened to endure it.

"And when he rose up from prayer… he said unto them, Why sleep ye? rise and pray, lest ye enter into temptation." (Luke 22:45–46)

And then:
"Rise up, let us go; lo, he that betrayeth me is at hand." (Mark 14:42)

No hesitation.

No resistance.

No retreat.

Prayer did not remove the assignment—

It empowered Him to complete it.

5. The Transformational Pattern for Us

Pray Under Pressure

Don't wait for calm—pray in crisis.

Pray Honestly

God can handle your real emotions.

Pray in Surrender

"Nevertheless" must be in every prayer.

Pray Until Strength Comes

Not until circumstances change—but until you change.

Chapter Reflection Questions

1. What "cup" are you asking God to remove?

2. Are you praying for escape—or strength?

3. Is "nevertheless" present in your prayers?

4. Are you spiritually willing but physically inconsistent?

Chapter Prayer

Father,

In moments of pressure, teach me to pray like Jesus.

Help me to be honest, yet submitted.

When I face things I do not want to endure, give me strength to say, "Nevertheless."

Align my will with Yours.

Prepare me through prayer for every assignment You have given me.

In Jesus' name, Amen.

Chapter 3

The Pattern of Prayer: Jesus on the Cross

Scripture Foundation (KJV)

"Then said Jesus, Father, forgive them; for they know not what they do. And they parted his raiment, and cast lots."
— Luke 23:34

"And at the ninth hour Jesus cried with a loud voice, saying, Eloi, Eloi, lama sabachthani? which is, being interpreted, My God, my God, why hast thou forsaken me?"
— Mark 15:34

"And when Jesus had cried with a loud voice, he said, Father, into thy hands I commend my spirit: and having said thus, he gave up the ghost."
— Luke 23:46

1. The Crushing Circumstances Surrounding the Prayer

Jesus is now on the cross.

Every prophecy is being fulfilled.

He has been:

- Betrayed
- Arrested
- Falsely accused
- Beaten beyond recognition
- Nailed to a cross

Scripture declares:

"But he was wounded for our transgressions, he was bruised for our iniquities…" (Isaiah 53:5)

The physical suffering was unbearable.

But the spiritual weight was even greater.

He bore:
- Every sin
- Every failure
- Every act of rebellion

And yet—He prayed.

They could strip Him of His clothes…

But they could not strip Him of His connection to the Father.

2. The Threefold Pattern of His Prayers

A. A Prayer of Forgiveness

"Father, forgive them; for they know not what they do."

This is shocking.

In the middle of injustice—

Jesus intercedes.

Not for relief.

But for forgiveness.

This sets up a divine pattern:

Prayer must include intercession—even for those who hurt you.

B. A Prayer of Identification with Humanity

"My God, my God, why hast thou forsaken me?"

This is not doubt—it is fulfillment.

"My God, my God, why hast thou forsaken me? why art thou so far from helping me…" (Psalm 22:1)

Jesus quotes prophecy.

In this moment, He experiences judicial separation because

He carries sin.

Yet notice—

He still says "My God."

Relationship remained, even in silence.

C. A Prayer of Surrender

"Father, into thy hands I commend my spirit…"

This is complete trust.

Jesus does not lose His life—

He releases it.

"No man taketh it from me, but I lay it down of myself…" (John 10:18)

This is the ultimate act of surrender.

3. The Outcome: Eternal Impact

Even in death—His prayer moved hearts.

"Now when the centurion saw what was done, he glorified God, saying, Certainly this was a righteous man." (Luke 23:47)

The cross was not defeat—it was fulfillment.

His prayers accomplished:

- Forgiveness released
- Prophecy fulfilled
- Redemption secured

4. The Transformational Pattern for Us

Pray When It Hurts Most

Your worst moment is still a prayer moment.

Pray for Others, Not Just Yourself

Even your enemies need your prayers.

Stay Connected to God in Silence

Even when you don't feel Him—He is there.

End in Surrender

Every prayer should end in trust.

Chapter Reflection Questions

1. Can you forgive those who hurt you deeply?

2. Have you ever felt God was distant? How did you respond?

3. Do you trust God enough to surrender everything?

4. What would change if you prayed even in your worst moments?

Chapter Prayer

Father,

Teach me to follow the pattern of Jesus.

Help me to forgive when it hurts, to trust when I don't understand, and to surrender completely.

Even in my darkest moments, keep my heart connected to You.

Let my life reflect the power of the cross through my prayer life.

In Jesus' name, Amen.

Chapter 4

The Priority of Prayer: The Daily Life of Jesus

Scripture Foundation (KJV)

"And in the morning, rising up a great while before day, he went out, and departed into a solitary place, and there prayed."
— Mark 1:35

"And it came to pass in those days, that he went out into a mountain to pray, and continued all night in prayer to God."
— Luke 6:12

"But he withdrew himself into the wilderness, and prayed."
— Luke 5:16

1. Prayer Was Not Occasional—It Was Foundational

One of the greatest misconceptions about prayer is that it is something we do only when we are in need. Whenever a crisis comes, we pray and cry out fervently to God. However, when we examine the life of Jesus, we discover that prayer was not His last resort—it was His first response. Prayer must be our lifestyle, part of our daily routine.

Jesus did not build His ministry on miracles.

He built His ministry on prayer.

Before the crowds came… He prayed.

Before decisions were made… He prayed.

Before power was demonstrated… He prayed.

Prayer was not something Jesus fit into His schedule—it was the foundation His schedule was built upon.

2. The Discipline of Early Prayer

"And in the morning, rising up a great while before day…" Jesus intentionally chose to meet with the Father before the demands of the day began.

This was not accidental—it was disciplined.

Early prayer represents:
• Priority
• Sacrifice
• Focus

Jesus gave God the first part of His day, not what was left over.

This challenges us deeply.

Many give God:
• The leftover energy
• The leftover time
• The leftover attention

But Jesus modeled something different:

God deserves first, not what remains.

3. The Necessity of Solitude in Prayer

"…and departed into a solitary place, and there prayed."

Jesus separated Himself.

He walked away from:
- Noise
- People
- Expectations

Not because people weren't important—but because connection with the Father was essential.

Solitude is not isolation—it is intentional separation for divine connection. Solitude offers an opportunity to shut out the distractions and focus on God.

In a world full of distractions, solitude has become rare.

But power is still found in private places.

Jesus Himself taught:

"But thou, when thou prayest, enter into thy closet, and when thou hast shut thy door, pray to thy Father which is in secret…" (Matthew 6:6)

The public power of Jesus was fueled by private prayer. Our foundation must be prayer.

4. The Consistency of Prayer

"And he withdrew himself into the wilderness and prayed." (Luke 5:16)

The wording here implies repetition.

This was not a one-time event.

Jesus had a pattern:

He often withdrew to pray.

Consistency is what transforms prayer from an event into a lifestyle.

Not:
- Occasional prayer
- Emergency prayer
- Crisis prayer

But:

Continual, consistent communion with God

5. The Depth of Extended Prayer

"And it came to pass in those days, that he went out into a mountain to pray, and continued all night in prayer to God." (Luke 6:12)

There are moments when prayer must go deeper.

Jesus prayed all night before making a major decision—the choosing of the twelve disciples.

This reveals a powerful principle:

The weight of the decision should determine the depth of the prayer.

Some things cannot be handled with casual prayer.

They require:
- Time
- Focus
- Intensely asking God for direction.

Power in God is always connected to lingering in prayer. Continuing to pray. Not just for a few moments but investing time into an activity that is vital to our lives.

THE WILDERNESS DISCIPLINE OF JESUS

Before Jesus preached publicly…

He prayed privately.

Before He healed publicly…

He battled privately.

Before He confronted demons…

He conquered Himself.

THE WILDERNESS IS NOT WASTED

"And Jesus being full of the Holy Ghost returned from Jordan, and was led by the Spirit into the wilderness."
— Luke 4:1

Notice:

The Spirit led Him there.

Not the devil.

The devil tempted Him there—

But the Spirit led Him there.

Sometimes God leads us into places of testing.

Not to destroy us.

But to reveal what is in us.

Wilderness seasons produce:

Dependence.

Discipline.

Discernment.

Depth.

Do not despise your wilderness.

God often does His deepest work in hidden places.

FASTING AND PRAYER

"And in those days he did eat nothing…"
— Luke 4:2

Jesus paired prayer with fasting.

Why?

Because fasting weakens flesh.

And what flesh loses—

Spirit gains.

Fasting does not manipulate God.

Fasting aligns us with God.

Some battles cannot be won casually.

Some breakthroughs require consecration.

Some victories require sacrifice.

FASTING AND PRAYER

"And in those days he did eat nothing…"
— Luke 4:2

Jesus paired prayer with fasting.

Why?

Because fasting weakens flesh.

And what flesh loses—

Spirit gains.

Fasting does not manipulate God.

Fasting aligns us with God.

Some battles cannot be won casually.

Some breakthroughs require consecration.

Some victories require sacrifice.

6. The Outcome: Power-Filled Living

After these moments of prayer, Jesus walked in undeniable authority.

"And they were all amazed, insomuch that they questioned among themselves, saying, What thing is this? what new doctrine is this? for with authority commandeth he even the unclean spirits, and they do obey him." (Mark 1:27)

His authority was not accidental or random—it was rooted in prayer.

7. The Transformational Pattern for Us

Make Prayer Your First Priority

Not your last choice.

Start Your Day with God

Before the world speaks—hear from heaven.

Create Space for Solitude

Disconnect from everything to connect with God.

Be Consistent

Prayer must become a lifestyle.

Go Deeper When Necessary

Some breakthroughs require extended prayer.

Chapter Reflection Questions

1. Is prayer your first response or your last resort?

2. What would change if you started every day with God?

3. Do you have a consistent place and time for prayer?

4. When was the last time you prayed beyond convenience?

Chapter Prayer

Father,

Teach me to prioritize prayer like Jesus did.

Help me to seek You early, consistently, and deeply.

Deliver me from casual prayer and draw me into committed communion.

Let my private time with You produce public power.

In Jesus' name, Amen.

Chapter 5

The Authority of Prayer: The Power in Jesus' Words

Scripture Foundation (KJV)

"And Jesus rebuked him, saying, Hold thy peace, and come out of him."
— Mark 1:25

"And when he had called his twelve disciples together, he gave them power and authority over all devils, and to cure diseases."
— Luke 9:1

"And whatsoever ye shall ask in my name, that will I do, that the Father may be glorified in the Son."
— John 14:13

1. Prayer Was the Source of Jesus' Authority

Jesus did not operate independently—He operated in alignment with the Father.

"Then answered Jesus and said unto them, Verily, verily, I say unto you, The Son can do nothing of himself, but what he seeth the Father do…" (John 5:19)

His authority flowed from:

- Relationship
- Submission
- Prayer

This is critical:

Authority in the Spirit is not self-generated—it is God-given. It's not how loud you speak, or how large your vocabulary is. God give you spiritual authority based upon your relationship with Him and time spent in prayer.

2. Authority Is Rooted in Alignment

Jesus only spoke what He heard from the Father.

"For I have not spoken of myself; but the Father which sent me, he gave me a commandment, what I should say, and what

I should speak." (John 12:49)

Prayer aligns us with heaven.

And when alignment happens—

Authority flows.

Many want authority without alignment.

But heaven only backs what heaven speaks.

3. The Demonstration of Authority Through Prayer

When Jesus spoke, things happened immediately.

"And Jesus rebuked him, saying, Hold thy peace, and come out of him." (Mark 1:25)

This was not a suggestion—it was a command.

And the result:

"And the unclean spirit, when he had torn him, and cried with a loud voice, came out of him." (Mark 1:26)

Authority speaks with confidence—not uncertainty. Authority speaks with assurance, knowing that God can take care of any situation we may face.

4. Authority Delegated to Believers

Jesus did not keep this authority to Himself.

"And when he had called his twelve disciples together, he gave them power and authority over all devils, and to cure diseases." (Luke 9:1)

This is transformational.

The same authority is available to believers who walk in alignment with God.

5. The Key: Praying in the Name of Jesus

"And whatsoever ye shall ask in my name, that will I do, that the Father may be glorified in the Son." (John 14:13)

Praying in Jesus' name is not a phrase—it is a position.

It means:

- Praying under His authority
- Praying according to His will
- Praying in alignment with His character

6. Authority Requires Faith and Fasting

Jesus revealed another layer of authority:
"And he said unto them, This kind can come forth by nothing, but by prayer and fasting." (Mark 9:29)

Some spiritual battles require deeper consecration.

Authority increases with:

- Prayer
- Fasting
- Obedience

7. The Outcome: Kingdom Power Manifested

Where authority is present:

- Demons flee
- Lives change
- Healing flows
- Freedom comes

Jesus declared:

"Behold, I give unto you power to tread on serpents and scorpions, and over all the power of the enemy…" (Luke 10:19)

8. The Transformational Pattern for Us

Stay Aligned with God

Authority flows from relationship.

Pray with Confidence

Not arrogance—but assurance.

Use the Name of Jesus Properly

Not casually, but with understanding and reverence.

Deepen Your Spiritual Discipline

Prayer and fasting unlock greater authority.

Chapter Reflection Questions

1. Are your prayers aligned with God's will?
2. Do you pray with confidence or hesitation?
3. What areas of your life need spiritual authority?
4. Are you willing to deepen your discipline through prayer and fasting?

Chapter Prayer

Father,

Align my heart with Yours.

Teach me to pray with authority, not fear.

Help me to walk in obedience so that heaven backs my words.

Increase my faith, deepen my discipline, and let Your power flow through my life.

In Jesus' name, Amen.

Chapter 6

The Intercession of Jesus: Praying for Others and Praying for Us

Scripture Foundation (KJV)

"Wherefore he is able also to save them to the uttermost that come unto God by him, seeing he ever liveth to make intercession for them."
— Hebrews 7:25

"I pray for them: I pray not for the world, but for them which thou hast given me; for they are thine."
— John 17:9

"But I have prayed for thee, that thy faith fail not: and when thou art converted, strengthen thy brethren."
— Luke 22:32

1. The Ministry of Intercession Defined

Intercession is more than prayer—it is standing in the gap.

It is:
• Praying on behalf of others
• Carrying burdens that are not your own
• Entering into spiritual labor for someone else's breakthrough

Jesus did not limit His prayer life to His own needs—He consistently prayed for others.

This reveals a critical truth:

A mature prayer life moves from selfish petitions to selfless intercession.

2. Jesus Prays for Peter: Personal Intercession

"But I have prayed for thee, that thy faith fail not…" (Luke 22:32)

Jesus knew Peter would fail.

He knew:
- The denial was coming
- The pressure would be intense
- The test would be overwhelming

Yet Jesus did not pray that Peter would avoid the test.

He prayed that Peter would survive it.

This is powerful truth for us to note.

God does not always remove the trial—

But He sustains you through it.

And then Jesus says:

"…and when thou art converted, strengthen thy brethren."

Your survival has purpose.

Your breakthrough is not just for you—

It is for those you will strengthen later.

3. The High Priestly Prayer: Jesus in John 17

John 17 is the most detailed recorded prayer of Jesus.

It is often called the **High Priestly Prayer.**

A. Jesus Prays for Himself (John 17:1–5)

"Father, the hour is come; glorify thy Son, that thy Son also may glorify thee." (John 17:1)

Even in praying for Himself, His focus was God's glory.

B. Jesus Prays for His Disciples (John 17:6–19)

"Holy Father, keep through thine own name those whom thou hast given me…" (John 17:11)

He prayed for:
• Their protection
• Their unity
• Their sanctification

"Sanctify them through thy truth: thy word is truth." (John 17:17)

C. Jesus Prays for Future Believers (That Includes Us)

"Neither pray I for these alone, but for them also which shall believe on me through their word." (John 17:20)
Jesus saw you.

Before you were born—

He prayed for you.

"That they all may be one…" (John 17:21)

4. Jesus' Ongoing Intercession

Jesus is still praying.

Right now.

"Who is he that condemneth? It is Christ that died, yea rather, that is risen again, who is even at the right hand of God, who also maketh intercession for us." (Romans 8:34)

This means:
- You are never alone
- You are never without covering
- You are never without advocacy

Jesus is your eternal intercessor. Hallelujah! That is a wonderful place to shout and thank God for His faithfulness.

5. The Power of Intercessory Prayer

Intercession changes:
- Lives
- Families
- Nations

"And I sought for a man among them, that should make up the hedge, and stand in the gap before me for the land..." (Ezekiel 22:30)

God is still looking for intercessors.

People willing to:
• Stand in the gap
• Carry the burden
• Pray until something shifts

6. The Transformational Pattern for Us

Pray for Others Regularly

Not just yourself.

Pray for Strength, Not Just Escape

Like Jesus did for Peter.

Pray for Future Generations

Your prayers will then outlive you.

Understand Jesus Is Praying for You

JESUS IS PRAYING RIGHT NOW!

This is not history.

This is present reality.

Jesus is alive.

Jesus is reigning.

Jesus is interceding.

Right now—

As you read this.

As you struggle.

As you fight.

As you cry.

As you believe.

Jesus is praying.

This means your failures are not final.

Your weakness is not permanent.

Your trial is not your ending.

Because heaven is speaking your name.

WHEN YOUR FAITH FEELS WEAK

"But I have prayed for thee…"
— Luke 22:32

Notice—

Jesus did not say:

"I prayed you would never struggle."

He said:

"I prayed your faith would not fail."

Faith may bend.

Faith may shake.

Faith may cry.

Faith may tremble.

But faith will not fail—

When Jesus is praying

Understand Jesus Is Praying for You

You are covered. You are not alone. You are not forgotten.

Chapter Reflection Questions

1. Who are you consistently praying for?

2. Are your prayers focused only on your needs?

3. Can you trust God to sustain others through trials instead of removing them?

4. How does it make you feel, knowing Jesus is praying for you?

Chapter Prayer

Father,

Give me the heart of an intercessor.

Teach me to carry others in prayer.

Help me to stand in the gap and pray with passion and persistence.

Thank You that Jesus is even now praying for me.

Let my life reflect that same love and commitment to others.

In Jesus' name, Amen.

Chapter 7

Living The Prayer Life of Christ: Transformation Through Application

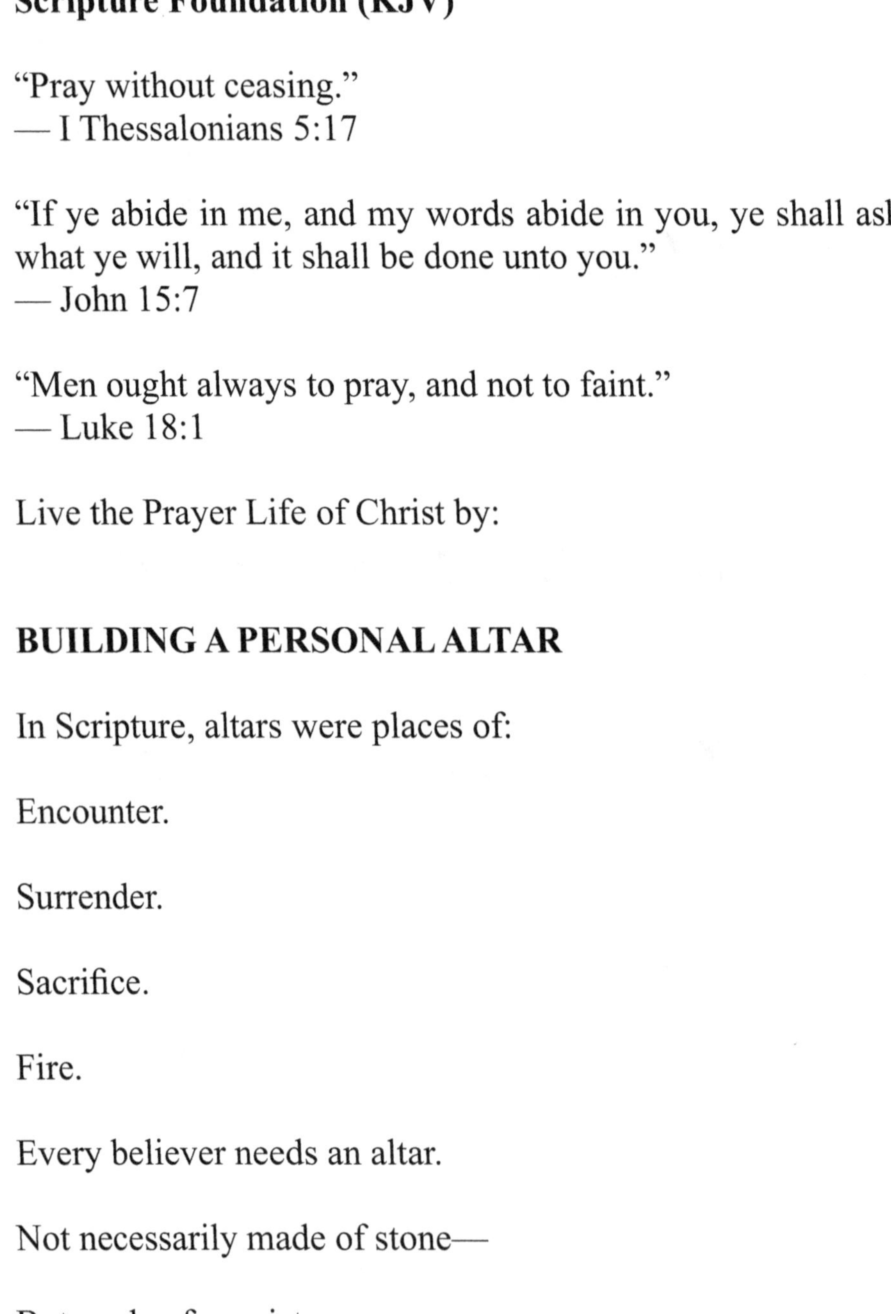

Scripture Foundation (KJV)

"Pray without ceasing."
— I Thessalonians 5:17

"If ye abide in me, and my words abide in you, ye shall ask what ye will, and it shall be done unto you."
— John 15:7

"Men ought always to pray, and not to faint."
— Luke 18:1

Live the Prayer Life of Christ by:

BUILDING A PERSONAL ALTAR

In Scripture, altars were places of:

Encounter.

Surrender.

Sacrifice.

Fire.

Every believer needs an altar.

Not necessarily made of stone—

But made of consistency.

A place.

A time.

A commitment.

A meeting place with God.

DEVELOPING A PRAYER JOURNAL

Write what God says.

Write what God reveals.

Write what God promises.

Write what God answers.

Because what gets written—
Gets remembered.

And what gets remembered—

Builds faith.

PRAYING IN THE HOLY GHOST

"But ye, beloved, building up yourselves on your most holy faith, praying in the Holy Ghost."
— The Holy Bible Jude 20

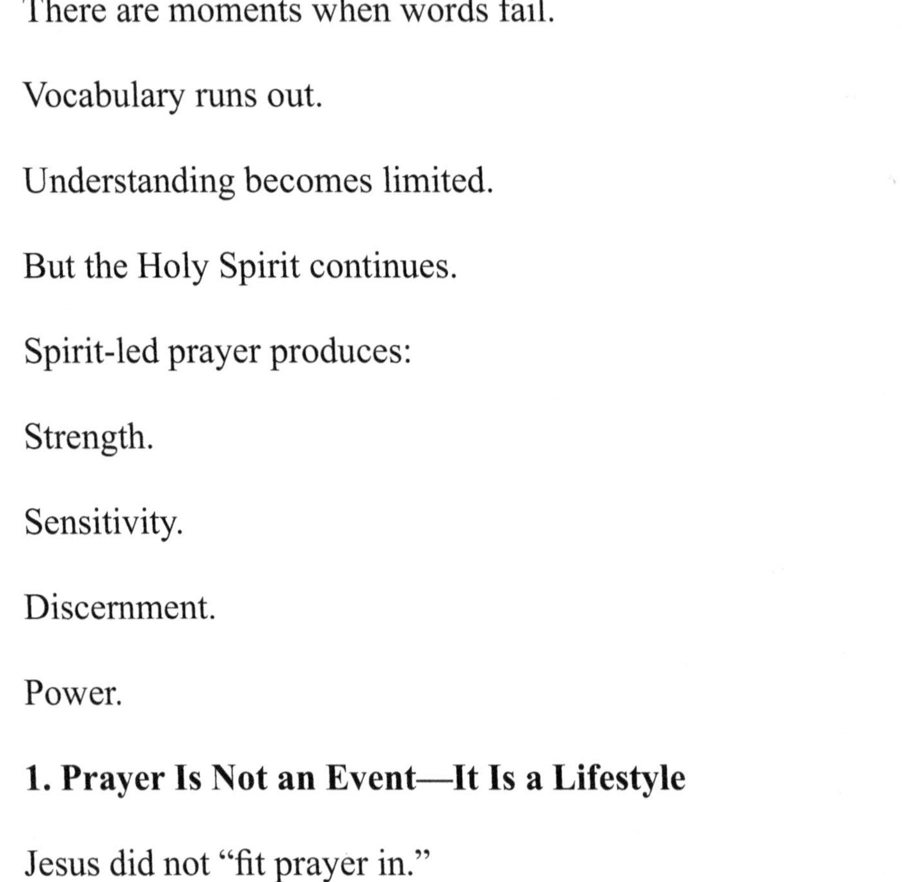

There are moments when words fail.

Vocabulary runs out.

Understanding becomes limited.

But the Holy Spirit continues.

Spirit-led prayer produces:

Strength.

Sensitivity.

Discernment.

Power.

1. Prayer Is Not an Event—It Is a Lifestyle

Jesus did not "fit prayer in."

He lived in prayer.

"Pray without ceasing." (I Thessalonians 5:17)

This does not mean nonstop talking—

It means continual awareness of God.

Prayer becomes:
- A mindset
- A posture
- A lifestyle

2. Abiding: The Key to Effective Prayer

"If ye abide in me, and my words abide in you…"

Abiding means:
- Remaining
- Staying connected
- Living in relationship

Prayer without relationship becomes routine.

But prayer with relationship becomes powerful.

3. Persistence in Prayer

"Men ought always to pray, and not to faint." (Luke 18:1)

Jesus taught persistence through the parable of the unjust judge.

The lesson:

Keep praying—even when answers delay.

Delay does not mean denial.

4. The Role of the Holy Spirit in Prayer

"Likewise the Spirit also helpeth our infirmities: for we know not what we should pray for as we ought…" (Romans 8:26)

The Holy Spirit:

- Guides prayer
- Strengthens prayer
- Intercedes through us

Power in prayer is given because of being Spirit-led in prayer.

5. Developing a Consistent Prayer Life

To live a prayer life like Jesus, we must be intentional.

A. Set a Time
Consistency builds strength.

B. Set a Place
Create a personal altar.

C. Set a Focus
Avoid distracted prayer.

6. Overcoming Prayer Obstacles

Common hindrances:

- Distraction

- Fatigue
- Doubt
- Busyness
- Lack of motivation to pray
- Feelings of inadequacy to even approach God

But Scripture reminds us:

"The effectual fervent prayer of a righteous man availeth much." (James 5:16)

7. The Outcome: A Transformed Life

When you pray like Jesus:

- Your perspective changes
- Your strength increases
- Your faith grows
- Your life aligns with God

Prayer is not just about changing things—

It changes you.

8. Final Call to Transformation

The question is not:

"Can you pray?"

The question is:

"Will you pray like Jesus?"

Chapter Reflection Questions

1. Is prayer a lifestyle or an occasional act for you?
2. Are you abiding in Christ daily?
3. What distractions hinder your prayer life?
4. What steps will you take to grow in prayer?

Chapter Prayer

Father,

Transform my prayer life.

Help me to live in constant connection with You.

Teach me to pray with persistence, power, and purpose.

Let my life reflect the pattern of Jesus.

From this day forward, let prayer become who I am—not just what I do.

In Jesus' name, Amen.

CONCLUSION

THE CALL TO A TRANSFORMED PRAYER LIFE

Prayer is not optional.

It is not reserved for the spiritually elite.

It is not limited to moments of crisis.

It is not confined to church buildings.

Prayer is the lifeline of every believer.

Throughout this book, we have walked through the prayer life of Jesus—not as spectators, but as students. We have examined His prayers in moments of:

- Grief at Lazarus' grave
- Agony in Gethsemane
- Sacrifice on the cross

We have seen His consistency, His authority, His intercession, and His unwavering connection to the Father.

And now we must answer one question:

What will we do with what we have learned?

1. The Example Is Clear

Jesus prayed:
- In public and in private
- In peace and in pressure
- In joy and in suffering

If Jesus—God in the flesh—prayed…

How much more do we need to pray?

"If my people, which are called by my name, shall humble themselves, and pray, and seek my face…"
— II Chronicles 7:14

Prayer is not a suggestion.

It is a command tied to promise.

2. Prayer Changes More Than Situations—It Changes You

Many approach prayer as a way to change circumstances.

But the deeper truth is:

Prayer transforms the person who prays.

Through prayer:
- Fear becomes faith

- Weakness becomes strength

- Confusion becomes clarity

- Flesh submits to Spirit

Jesus did not leave Gethsemane with a different assignment—He left with strengthened resolve.

3. The Three Questions That Define Your Prayer Life

As you move forward, continually ask:

What are the circumstances around me?

Where is prayer needed right now?

What is the substance of my prayer?

Is it:
- Faith-filled?

- God-centered?

- Spirit-led?

What outcome do I expect?

Do I genuinely believe God will respond?

4. Remember It is A Lifestyle, not a Moment

"Pray without ceasing." — I Thessalonians 5:17

This is not about constantly speaking—

It is about constantly staying connected.

Prayer becomes:

- Your first response
- Your steady rhythm
- Your daily foundation

5. The Final Challenge

Don't read this book and remain the same.

Now you must decide:

Will you:
- Pray occasionally?

- Or pray consistently?

Will you:
- Pray casually?

- Or pray with power?

Will you:
- Pray your will?

- Or surrender to God's will?

6. The Invitation

God is not distant.

He is not unwilling.

He is not silent toward those who seek Him.

"Call unto me, and I will answer thee, and shew thee great and mighty things, which thou knowest not."
— Jeremiah 33:3

The invitation is open.

The access has been granted.

The example has been given.

Final Prayer
Father,

Thank You for the example of Jesus.
Teach us to pray with power, purpose, and pattern.
Draw us into deeper relationship with You.
Let our prayer lives be transformed from routine to revival.
Use our prayers to impact our homes, our churches, and our world.
From this moment forward, we commit to seeking You like never before.

In Jesus' name, Amen.

Personal Thoughts

Personal Thoughts

Personal Thoughts

Personal Thoughts

Personal Thoughts

Personal Thoughts

Personal Thoughts

Personal Thoughts

Personal Thoughts

Plan of Salvation

How You Can Receive Jesus Christ As your Lord And Savior

If you would like to welcome Jesus Christ into your life, you can do so at any time, anywhere.

Consider these important facts:

God loves you and seeks a personal relationshp with you! "Behold, I stand at the door and knock. If anyone hears My voice and opens the door, I will come in to him and dine with him, and he with Me."

Revelation 3:20

The problem is: Everyone has been born into this world spiritually dead because of sin.

"For the wages of sin is death, but the gift of God is eternal life in Christ Jesus our Lord."

Romans 6:23

Jesus will forgive us of all sin, assuring us of eternity in Heaven! "If we confess our sins, he is faithful and just to forgive us our sins and to cleanse us from all unrighteousness."

1 John 1:9

To receive Jesus, pray this prayer:

Lord Jesus, I'm a sinner. Please come into my life and forgive me of all sin. I believe You died for my sins and rose from the dead. Now, fill me with Your Holy Spirit and guide me from this day forward. Thank you, Lord, for saving me! **Amen!**

Biography

Sonjia B. Dickerson

Pastor Sonjia B. Dickerson *is a powerhouse of purpose, faith, and leadership!*

She's not just in ministry — she is called to it. With a voice that moves nations and a heart that nurtures souls, she spends her time shaping lives, building vision, and advancing the Kingdom of God.

As Executive Pastor of Dayspring Family Church in Irving, Texas, she leads with her husband, Bishop Kevin Keith Dickerson, stewarding a thriving ministry that reflects excellence, empowerment, and Spirit-filled worship. But her impact stretches far beyond her local church.

She is a global voice, having preached nationally and internationally for over 30 years, carrying the mantle of revival, healing, deliverance, and divine wisdom. She is the founder and CEO of the Outpouring Women's Conferences, which impact thousands of women annually, in and outside of the state of Texas.

As the visionary behind C.L.A.S.S., Inc. (Cultivating Leaders Achieving Scholastic Success), a nonprofit that develops leaders and funds the dream of college attendance for high school graduates, she is literally changing destinies. With over 250 college scholarships awarded (and counting), it is evident that Pastor Sonjia believes in education, in opportunity, and in giving the next generation the support and push they need to move forward.

Pastor Sonjia has not only written 11 books and recorded five music projects, but she has also obtained a Bachelor's Degree in Accounting from Loyola University in Chicago, Illinois, a Master's Degree in Biblical Studies, a Doctor of Ministry from Vision International University, and a Masters of Christian Leadership from Criswell College. She currently serves on various community boards and is the leader who other leaders look to for clarity, conviction, and courage.

Pastor Sonjia balances family and ministry with grace. She is married to her sweetheart, Bishop Kevin Dickerson. They have two daughters, one son, a bonus son-in-love and a daughter-in-love. They are also the proud grandparents of five precious grandchildren.

Whether she is teaching about self-discipline, prayer, dominion, or hope, Pastor Sonjia Dickerson always delivers God's word with truth, love, wisdom and power.

Sonjia B. Dickerson Ministries

Now Available for

ENGAGEMENTS

Preacher Teacher Singer Author

Conferences

Revivals

Concerts

Workshops

Podcast Guest

etc...

Booking Info:

outpouringwc@gmail.com

@pastorsonjia

Follow me on Facebook

www.ingramcontent.com/pod-product-compliance
Lightning Source LLC
LaVergne TN
LVHW020646100826
845148LV00012B/2349

* 9 7 8 1 7 3 3 0 2 3 5 8 0 *